PREFACE

This collection of poetry was written for the purposes of bringing about more awareness in regards to hidden disabilities. To be more specific, this collection uses a variety of creative writing techniques to portray a small sense of the internal struggles of those who suffer from chronic or long-term illnesses that others cannot see.

I myself suffer from fibromyalgia and it has not been an easy journey. I always described myself as a work-a-holic, i could never have imagined before being diagnosed that my body could one day refuse to keep pace with me. In the last two years i have worked hard to pace myself and discover the previously seemingly-hidden networks that are out there for those who suffer from similarly debilitating conditions.

If you could take one thing from this collection, i'd like it to be the knowledge that there is always someone out there who will listen, don't lock yourself away when you are struggling. So many of us have hidden lives.

CONTENTS

HIDDEN LIVES

Shanel Chalmers

SHE'S LOOKING AT ME

She's looking at me,

That woman. Name badge too far to read.

She eyes me as if I'm pocketing something,

I am.

Pocketing it up, pushing it right down.

I'm carrying as much as I physically can.

A touch of Tramadol -

Lightening the load.

She snarls as I go for the handle. Pounces.

Chiselled claws flawlessly painted,

They scratch my periphery.

"Excuse me!" She exclaims.

"This is for disabled! Can't you read?"

Her smile stretches across the store.

"I am" I Whisper. She looks me up and down,

"You look fine to me."

MAKING MASKS

A stitched smile, its paint newly drying -

Over tears that had bubbled the surface.

Time to put yesterday's mask aside,

Into the draw it goes with the others.

Crossing out each calendar box,

Painting over each yesterday as they come.

I'm looking more and more the part.

Mannequin fingers, whitening and numb, -

I stitch the lines I'd like to see.

I make myself, re-paint whatever I don't like, something –

I can control. The way my face doesn't show it,

The trickling pain coursing me, the struggle.

I must keep the tears from bubbling a fresh coat,

Stitched smile underneath, newly drying on my skin.

I cover the epidermal lines that tell their own story.

I can forget the scars beneath with a smile.

I won't speak of it, I won't need to –

If I paint over it again.

WHAT DO YOU SEE?

What do you see in her enigma? Her puzzle-box body?

What do you see beneath the occasion crook of her spine, -

Or the spontaneous gasp of her breath?

Do you see a struggle? A battlefield?

Or just another body not unlike your own?

I've learnt not to trust my eyes. They mislead even me.

I look in the mirror now and then and see a body –

Not unlike your own. But it misleads even me.

I see legs and arms, no defect or missing pieces.

What do I see in her enigma, she –

Who stares back at me? Skin paled in pain perhaps?

But she misleads with her pretence of physical capacity.

Its skin deep, not muscle and tissue penetrating, but surfaced.

Beneath her pipes are bursting, waters flooding, -

But there are no pot holes on her surface, no signs of flooding out.

A bottled-body filled up as much as it can take.

What do you see? Her standing at the roadside looking breathless,

Just a jogger, or the cold perhaps has stripped her lungs of stretch.

Do you see a struggle? The possibility of your eyes misleading even you, -

A frightening thought that control is not always our own.

She is a solitary battlefield, but she is not alone.

THE WEIGHT OF
A DAISY CHAIN

Vibrant green around my neck, they'll notice.

Brightly yellowed petals pointedly painted, -

Like little knives they poke out in all directions.

Defence.

Now they see me. The store clerk –

Flinging shopping across the counter like he's bowling.

There go the apples, likely bruising beneath their skin.

He notices.

Asks me if I'd like help packing. It takes a chain around my neck -

For him to notice the subtle shake of my hand, stutter in my voice.

I nod feeling guilty for wrapping myself in a label.

I need this.

The shake in my hand worsens, he notices. The chain pulls against my skin.

I am more aware of myself, my incapability, the room spinning around me.

He asks if I'm okay. I smile as if I am.

I smile.

He packs the bag for me, offers me a hand to the car. He sees the badge in the window.

I've done it. Gained some independence without uttering a word. But,

It's hard to breathe under the weight of a daisy chain.

WHEELCHAIR
IN THE RIVER

I tossed my wheelchair in the river,

Watched it float downstream.

The fishes love swimming around it,

Finding a home against my shadowed indentations.

A need I do not want.

Sitting on a little bridge watching the sparkle of the waters,

A swerve and flow I cannot mimic.

Fishes ignoring my presence.

My legs edged over the side, water around my toes,

I feel the way it looks - swirling around me.

A couple passes, smiles, comments on the wheelchair.

How it's lodged on some rocks, weathering quickly –

Against the flow of water.

Wheels wedged, stationary, perhaps its feeling my resignation.

A need I do not want.

YOU LOOK FINE

I look fine, I must admit, with my hair brushed up in a ponytail.

You cannot see the layers of dry shampoo that have yet to form a skin.

I look fine, I do not contest it, with my makeup almost worthy of a YouTube tutorial.

Fresh faced and un-paled with a three-shade darker foundation than my skin.

I look fine because my clothes are washed by my carer but how would you know.

Because I look fine.

Yes, I do not step outside my door on those days my legs won't take me down the stairs,

I do not leave my comfortable four walls.

I look fine, more so than some, on days when my carer helps me put on socks and do up shoes.

I do look fine.

I do not hide my world from you, you do not ask. I do not wish to tell so we are equally agreed to say-

I do look fine – today.

DECOMPOSING

I watch her decomposing, the weight of her body changing,-

Muscles weakening, eyes softening in giving in.

Unable to soundly sleep. Her face haunting,

Alongside the pain of letting go.

Now she has decomposed beyond recognition,

A memory. I cannot see her reflecting back any longer.

Her light smile drooped and misshapen. Her eyes blackened.

She is no longer me. Decomposed beyond mourning,

Words I cannot breathe along my tongue-

For fear that they are real.

Have I lost her so entirely? She,-

A whirlwind of energy, reduced to stagnation.

Pain, a crippling foe, murderess without specification.

Have I lost her so entirely?

BENEATH THE SURFACE

The surface sheet of the sea glints back at me,

Sparkling like the diamond-edged refraction of light.

Blue and pink like the veins lining my thin-skinned arms.

Nothing else is visible.

I push my hands along the water,

The cold burns my fingers. The pain is refreshingly new.

I watch for something underneath to move,-

Hoping to see more hidden there, but I do not.

My body submerges further off the side of the little boat,

It teeters to and fro with my indecision.

Sink or swim, as if floating is not an option.

I search for middle ground.

The sun warms my skin to a blister,

My eyes refuse to open,-

Behind them there is scratching.

The smell of salt heavying the air, squeezing-

My lungs for space.

Do I dare to peek beneath the surface,-

Dare to see more than I'd wish.

As if I am an iceberg, for that is what frightens me.

Do I dare to visage what's beneath?

THE MASKS
WE MAKE

The little intricacies in the masks we make, refinements-

So subtle that each is entirely its own.

Like finger prints, we all have them, defining our singularity.

A way to feel safe, a masking of pain.

For we are mask makers, creators of a soft diversity-

Of sifting souls hiding behind knowledge that masks make us feel safe.

We are crafters of personas, aficionados of the word fine.

Both puppet and puppeteer.

But masks are breakable things, they fray and wrinkle in time.

They require much care.

Plaster, paint, re-paint, add or drop a stitch. Widening a smile-

Or yellowing out the black under each eye

Masking the pain that's painted clearly on the face beneath,

The masks we make to hide what lies beneath.

HIDDEN IN
THE WALLS

One day when you are older, tear down the walls to make this space
your home,

For every brick we laid, we laid for you to make your own.

The first I laid for you my son, and another for another.

Your father laid a brick by mine, we found home within each other.

Believe me when I tell you son, I wanted for you the very best,

But my body won't allow me now to do much more than rest.

When you are grown, and I am old, there will be hope still hidden-

In the walls we built together, in the love that we had given.

The way the corridors curve, doors at intervals like notches on a
spine.

Laughter still running through these subtle curves of mine.

But, we cannot stay much longer, the stairs are far too much to
bare,

And although our world is changing and it doesn't feel so fair-

I laid a brick once by a brick your father laid,

Together we built walls around us, in which I wish we could have
stayed.

For that I am sorry son, that I have no the strength to stand,

Perhaps if I were built of bricks my body would not act like sand.

But, hidden in the walls is hope, the hope that you will make your
own-

This space your father and I once called our home.

I cannot promise you that you will find the memories you are look-
ing for-

In the patterns ingrained into the wooden floors.

But, when I look at the curling staircase, the ceiling stretching
   high,

The way I had imagined it if my body could defy.

I mourn the loss of greater things, of steady hands and feet,

For me our home is now just another house upon a street.

One day when you are older, tear down the walls to make this space
   your home,

For every brick we laid, my son, we laid for you to make your own.

◆ ◆ ◆

THE SAME FOUR WALLS

My friend stopped on my doorstep & rang the bell impatiently.
She held in her hands the latest catalogue of some place or another,
A Christmas prepping enthusiast. She looked -
Down the dark corridor,
And asked me why?
The lights weren't on.
Of course they weren't!
No one comes to see the corridor.
Why bother anymore? She made herself at home.
She handed me the catalogue, clicked the kettle on for two,
Made herself a crease in the yellow had-seen-better-days settee.
She looked comfortable, more so than I had in some time, refreshed-
By the blackout blinds concealing the hot glare of a summer's afternoon.
She took her coat off but quickly redressed herself with a rub or two of her arms.
Soon it was time for her to go. A smile, a wave, a fondness I had come to know
On such an occasion. Next week lingered on my tongue. I looked at the clock,
Clicked the kettle on for one. Let the lights flicker out throughout.
Soon no sound could be heard, even the wind was dead.
And in a *few* more days perhaps, the postman-
He might come and ring the bell
Impatiently. Or not.

SILENCE

There is a silence in forced smiling.

A cry that goes unheard.

It goes without need for questions,

Not acknowledged as having any right to cry at all.

Behind blue bottle-shaken eyes,-

The sadness of a quiet cry leads to bed.

There is no hand to hold,-

There is silence there instead.

There is something dark behind forced smiles.

A cry going unheard, without witness,

A crime that no one knows.

They're not acknowledged as having any rights at all.

As if crying could have a bigger purpose,

Could turn a head or two.

There is a silence in forced smiling,

But that's what I'm used to.

REVERBERATING

Can you hear me? Cries a little voice beneath my bed that I ignore.

Can you hear me? It calls in the dead of night.

I am sure it is waiting for something, its fingers tap impatiently,

But I do not response.

Can you hear me? Softly settles on the air around me, warm and sweet,

The smell of summer nights and crushed almonds in the kitchen,

Someone baking cake, it lingers.

Can you hear me? Like a soft whistle, gentle and breathless it calls.

Can you hear me? Cries a little voice beneath my bed that I ignore,

Until it makes no sound, not anymore.

Are you there? I whisper to the quiet space beneath my bed,

To the darkness, a dropped sweet-wrapper den.

Are you there? I whisper for another night, relentlessly testing the silence,

Shaking it to see if it cracks. But, there are no noises coming from my bed.

I wrap the sheets around myself, alone and cold, wondering.

What did the little voice want with its softly spoken 'can you hear me?

MY TRANSLUCENCE

I aim for translucency despite the things I hide,

For honesty despite continued lies –

Like I'm okay. I have good intentions,

When I say I'm doing well.

Trying hard to hide-

Behind a shell that I have made for myself.

I cannot seem to give the care I need,

Sometimes it's hard enough to feed-

The body that is me.

And so I lie,

Because I've tried-

Every idea I could fathom not to hide,

But the reality will not subside to my attempts.

I do still care,

Smewhere deep within my skin,

That I don't see, I only feel-

The post-traumatic horror that I feel is me.

And so I lie,

Because it's easier to say -

That you're okay, pretend,

And hold yourself together for another day.

Push down those feelings of falling -

From tall places, empty spaces,

As if these feelings aren't encasing, aren't racing –

Through my head.

The thought that I'm already dead,

Words I find myself repeating-

To my psychiatrist instead of you.

Am I dead?

For despite my continued lies-

I have tried to lift myself from my bed-

Like I'm okay.

When my tongue tangles in my throat,

Breathing becomes blue and un-emote,

The things I should be telling you-

All catching in my throat.

And this pain feels never ending,

Unrelenting, only medication-bending

To a degree.

And so I lie,

Because a lie isn't real, isn't existing

In the space in which I'm sitting.

Against my teeth, it isn't gritting.

When I say that I'm okay, that I'm fine,

well I'm lying.

But, I'm trying to be translucent

Despite the pain I'm clearly hiding.

And so I lie.

NO MORE LIES

You do not need to lie to yourself for me,

I will believe that you are struggling if you say.

You need not paint it white to protect me,

It does not need to be black and blue, shouted-

Because you are scared I will not understand.

I do not need to feel the pain that you are in.

Your lie may be yellowed and flaking,

Like an unloved or well-loved book,

It may be brown. Washed down in heavy rain,

Cold and hurtful in its truth, when you say-

That I won't understand. It is okay.

I do not need to feel the pain that you are in.

You do not need to lie to yourself for me,

Pretend that you can stand if you cannot,-

I will not question you. Sit and rest,

Good friend, I will not pretend to understand.

Keep your lies for days when you wish to be alone,

To hide hurtful truths from yourself but not from me.

Your lie may be a red and raw gaping wound,

It may sting to hear and rattle in my ears until they are sore.

But I will not tell you you'll be fine, chin up, just smile.

I will not downplay the turning of your body,

On and off, setting itself anew with mismatched circuitry.

Friend, you do not need to pretend. I will believe it if you say.

I WHISPER

I whisper in the dark, tongue twitching, hoping to be heard.

Needing to be alone. It's complicated.

I whisper please help and hope –

That you don't answer.

Stay my personal-space away.

It's a great defiance you see - not to be touched.

Passers-by in long coats, thick soled shoes,-

They do not notice.

I am content with the way these things have been,

A solitary safety in daily repetitions of this scene,

Please help me another whisperer calls and I ignore.

I hadn't noticed him before.

His hair defies gravities weighing-down, it flails,

I watch. It's thickly coated in something, oil, grease, dirt, some-
thing.

If he's hiding a smile he's hiding it well.

His body malnourished, eyes absently blinking.

I whisper help? His head turns, clicks as it does, and fixes on me.

Something behind his eyes moves, a tear perhaps.

His ears glow bright red, the cold or the shock of being heard, -

I am not certain to the cause.

We sit together, I am shocked at my willingness to be this close.

He edges over, he is cold, his bones rattling beneath his coat.

MRS SHANEL CHALMERS M.A.

I put my hands out for us both

I whisper please help and hope –

INVISIBLE ME

She stands in her purple shawl reading beautifully,

Knowing others cannot see how exhausted she may be-

Simply reading from a page, thinking straight-

For the length of day this day will surely take.

Beneath her skin are multiple facsimiles of M and E,

She stands with grace despite herself – for me.

She does not waver, tilt, nor lean.

Her intent remaining keen - to do it right.

She reads with all the justice she has learned-

And feels the sense of pride that she has earned,

It builds it way around the room in an applause.

This is her queue and so she withdraws.

Flowers stitched across her shoulders, silver threads,

Printed dress to contrast her as guest.

She closes her eyes and feels the moments pass,

Her strength endures though her body feels like glass.

Her face beams, a glow of blushed-rose, softer now.

She wraps herself in her shawl, a comfort. She can now allow-

Herself to rest, and relish in the task that's passed.

The beauty in her words heard at last.

I MIGHT BE MORE

My mother looks at me, sharp jawed, thick chinned.

The space between her eyes seems to be growing.

Her mouth twitches at its corners, lips thinly pursed.

Her voice, a low hiss, building to coherence.

"You might've been more, you know, if you'd married,-

If you'd had children they could've looked after you."

I hear the words *instead of me* float silently between us,

Her nose turning blue as she bottles in the words she wants to say.

"You might've been more", she whistles beneath her breath.

She leaves me to my room, an empty space I am accustomed to.

"I might've been more" I repeat. Is it a mantra or a spell? If I repeat-

Will my legs begin to move, will I grow, will I explode?

The way my mother looked at me as if I wasn't more, already-

I lift my arms in defiance of my bodies will. I will not rest,

So I compose a litany, a prayer – though my legs don't move,

I will not rest until I prove I might be more.

My mother enters an empty room, the smell of me lingering,

Sweet decay of scent she once wished to wash away.

I am not under the crinkled covers stretched across the little bed,

I am not by the window I could never reach.

My mother looks for me, sharp jawed, thick chinned.

The space between her eyes seems to be growing,

She is showing some remorse. She cannot hide me on her face,

Though she had tried.

My mother's soft hands place themselves against the covers,

Her legs rest until they're numb. She cannot move,

And when she tries she finds the exhaustion is too much-

That she must lay.

The sheets are cotton, a soft pink. Camomile-scented for me,

Heavy, so I barely breathe while I'm asleep. Had she hoped-

There would be no more of me. The morning rose its head,

She jolts upright in my bed, a scream she cannot scream.

I might be more than a memory to her now, as she lifts-

To find no lift left in her frame. Parts of her no longer work the
same.

A scream she cannot scream. Sat on my bed, an empty space,

She should be accustomed. She is not.

I look at my mother, sharp jawed and thick chinned.

My eyes void of caring yet I am pulled to her side.

"You might've been more you know", I whisper

"You might've even been a mother had you tried".

HAD I A CHANCE?

It all goes black so frequently, the colour stripping itself back,

I cannot see. This, I don't remember when I wake.

It's like a dream, the world is here and then it's gone.

My eyes open, body on the washing pile, not knowing-

Where the time has gone.

I worry, being left alone, waking on the floor.

Did I fall down the stairs this time? Did I hit my head?

Should I take myself to bed?

Everyone repeating *you need to rest* as if sitting still is easy,

Doing nothing is a test of my sanity, a jest, surely.

Then, I opened the car door, face feeling the window first, then the
floor.

Eyes open to my husband holding me, rain falling,-

Body colder than before. Hands are cut,

I don't feel the blood rush out, I see red dripping from the door

I don't remember the before.

It all goes black so frequently, this macabre inexplicability,

It tethers me to my bed. Had I a chance of knowing before I go-

That I'm going, but I don't remember the before.

I'm resigned to never knowing, no choice in overflowing-

When and wherever I'm going, to the blankness of before.

PULLED BACK
TO BED

Her body holds a poltergeist that pulls her back to bed,

Sometimes it throws her here and there, banging both her limbs
and head.

Her body holds a poltergeist that throws things from her hands,

It screams at her deep scratching screams, whatever it demands?

She doesn't understand why her body's not her own,

She questions what she's done, but the answers still unknown.

Her body holds a poltergeist, it whispers in her ear-

A loud sounding static noise that she's begun to fear.

Her body holds a poltergeist, one no one else can see,

The doctors can't explain it, label it fibro or ME.

She takes their medications, the therapies they throw,

Jumps through the hoops the doctors hold but it only seems to
grow.

Her body holds a poltergeist, she's trying hard not to give in,

She knows she can't escape, there's only co-existing.

Her body holds a poltergeist that pulls her back to bed,

And if she goes willingly it cries soft cries instead.

A CAFFEINATING STRENGTH

She wakes me with a sharp stab to my nostrils,

A bitter inhale at first light.

I roll my hands around her rounded edges.

She's what gets me through the mornings.

She, a comfortable blend from Italy,

Caramelised, not too strong.

I intend to fill her to a brim,-

Enjoying the strength she gives me as I sit-

Helplessly waiting.

Pain settles in my lower back, it is sharp.

The thought of going out grows bitter.

Pain has its way, it makes me need another.

Sweet caramel bringing me back, I lose my words.

They trail from me, linger atmospherically,

Mocking the disturbance in my faculty.

I push back in my wooden chair, feel the teeter of my little table,

Grab the saucer to stop the shake.

I hold my shot of caramel, shot of morphine to the pain.

I let my lips sit on the edge, a yellowed porcelain,

It gets me through the day. It's sharp.

The pain in my lower back, it wakes me.

FRIEND HOLDING ME UP

I opened out my hand to see that cut. We thought blood oaths were
so cool-

When we were back in school and causing trouble round the block.

Our mothers left us to our devices, we rode bicycles back and forth
to the shops,

They weren't always our own, how could we have known it wasn't
cool.

We were only young in school, and though I know it's obvious to
you-

It's an excuse, to us it was of use to burn off adolescence fast.

We'd hoped the awkward stages wouldn't last too long, didn't
think-

That round the corner were taxes, driving schools, more rules.

We didn't know the world was cruel, that we weren't going to be
cool, till it was a little late.

My face was left a slate, looking the fool, stood aside your bed.

I opened out my hand to see that cut. We thought blood oaths were
so cool-

I didn't know that you'd get sick, that our bodies were full of rules
like keep it in.

Your arm was a watercolour palette from arts class, the ones that
didn't last very long.

The ones we mostly threw or broke apart. Anything for a laugh.

I didn't know we'd end up here with you too asleep to feel the
things I fear.

Our mums came quick, they sat by your side till dinner time,

Then there were the other kids to think about. I wouldn't move.

My mum dragged me from your room insisting I get home soon to get some sleep.

As if I could, with you lying all alone somewhere I couldn't telephone,

Because you couldn't pick up from your bed, so the line would have gone dead.

Mum lights a candle this time of year, as if she's keeping you alive.

She doesn't mention you for fear of what she might let rise in me, a tear,

Or something more she cannot see. I lay in my old room thinking of you,

How we thought we were so cool, how we wouldn't be mundane.

I work in an office now, I barely do a job. It's a file, delete, repeat – kind of world.

Sometimes I cry, sometimes I'm too drunk to see what's going on inside,

I'd rather hide away. Back in my room, where we grew up, well I grew up.

And you, you haunt me in the photographs that line my walls,

The happy smile that isn't there anymore. You haunt me.

I look down at my hand to see that scar, wishing it was me that went too far.

◆ ◆ ◆

KINDNESS LIKE I'VE NEVER KNOWN

A kindness like I've never known has come from this,

The pieces of myself that I'd thought broken.

Kindness in another way of life, holding myself up,

Listening to my pains that otherwise I leave to go unspoken.

A kindness growing from a deep sense of loss.

Comparing the incapability's of who I am now.

I am a rot of sorts, once the rose and now whatever feeds off its decay.

I am the rot, and all the opportunity that being something else might thus allow.

A kindness in changing, a butterfly reversion, I sink deep within my shell.

I am growing against the grain, a different way.

I am kinder for it, eyes softer, hands more open to reaching out.

I am the rot. I acknowledge it without delay.

My petals may have curled, strength fallen inward,

My colours may have faded with my scent.

Now, I am the rot that holds my former body-

To rent, and by doing so another day my life is lent.

Easier to accept what I am now then hate what's new,

I cannot revert my body's ways. I can still choose,

However, whether I am something greater than before.

Despite my former life, I am the rot, I shall endure.

IN THE HIDDEN LIVES WE GROW

I am eased by the people that I know, every shape and race,

Born from every place. Sitting around a table we grow.

Chairs already placed, table fully laced in welcoming embrace, it's why I go.

None of us had chosen to be this way, some are friendlier than others,

Some struggle more. He falls, she stands tall, he is confident but she-

Shies from all adversity for somewhere else she'd rather be.

But still she comes and always speaks so pleasantly,

For even she does not wish to be alone.

He has a dog to comfort him, she has a child or two. He-

Is made of stronger stuff but it's clear he's suffering too.

We each have a story, something to hold and own,

But we come together at this table to not feel so alone.

The coffee is ready, the tea is brewing in the pot,-

There's always a helping hand when yours is shaking, sometimes it's not.

She pours me a drink, smiles, *how's your day?* I return her smile-

Not knowing what to say.

I do not wish to confess I've only just gotten out of bed,

That my legs have muscle spasms, and walking gives me dread.

She puts a hand on my shoulder. *It's okay*, she smiles,-

And, the softness in her voice makes me feel it for a while.

It's okay to not be okay, it's okay to feel as though you're falling-

When you're here. No one is calling out for you to smile, put a face on for a while.

It's okay not to be okay, it's not a crime.

So, *take your time.* I tell myself when I walk in. *It's okay.* No one's judging me-

My body trembles less, the pain faded back, all I think about is coffee in the pot.

I sit down, not uncomfortable in any spot.

Gotten used to *how's your day?* And now I'm the one to say-

It's been okay. Growing in the knowledge that I'm not alone,

Scraping the surface, a little more each time I'll know-

Of the Hidden Lives we grow.

Printed in Great Britain
by Amazon